And He Sent Them Forth

**And how shall they preach, except they be sent?...
Romans 10:15a**

Pearl Ballew Jenkins

A Great Love, Inc.
Toccoa, Georgia

Unless otherwise indicated, all scriptural quotations are from the *King James Version* of the Bible.

And He Sent Them Forth
ISBN 0-929263-04-9
Copyright © 1990 by
A Great Love, Inc.
P.O. Box 1248
Toccoa, GA 30577

Published by
A Great Love, Inc.
P.O. Box 1248
Toccoa, GA 30577
U.S.A.

Contents

Acknowledgments

A special thanks to Eva Benevento for her gracious help in editing the manuscript of this book. I also want to acknowledge and thank Fay Dease, who did some typing for me, and Aubrey Phillips for his assistance in reviewing the material and writing a foreword. In addition, I wish to express my heart-felt gratitude and appreciation to Bobbie Jean Merck and A Great Love, Inc., for getting the book printed and making it possible for it to reach the readers much sooner than I could have done. To God be the Glory!

— Pearl Ballew Jenkins

Foreword

I first met the author of this book, Pearl Ballew Jenkins, when I was a newly converted teenager in Calcutta, India. That was many years ago. This elegant lady was tall, slim, good looking, well groomed, and had fine wavy brown hair. But what was most impressive (and at my age at that time I was most impressionable) was her charm, her graciousness, and her deep spirituality. She seemed to know God so intimately, and had a closeness with God that I envied.

I met her at a Christian friend's apartment and subsequently at the two churches I attended. She was a Miss Sahib (unmarried missionary lady) and kept appearing and disappearing from time to time as I recall. I learned that she had a mission station in Puri, a seaside town located on the Bay of Bengal, and she went back and forth from her center there on ministry calls.

Time and circumstance brought me on a convalescent visit to her place in Puri at her invitation. It was there that I met the Linden family, Pentecostal missionaries to India, whose daughter later became my wife. The Lindens invited me to spend a few months with them in the mountains neighboring Landour (a missionary hill station in the Himalayas) which I accepted. They were planning an evangelistic trip into the mountain villages. Pearl joined us on this mission and we all had some memorable times together in prayer, fellowship, preaching in the vernacular (even I had a go at this, somewhat inexpertly), and walking the mountains. By the end of this venture, we had all become firm friends, and have remained so through the years.

I remember Pearl praying with compassion and agony for the spiritually darkened Hindu people of the hill villages. She also prayed for me with equal fervency. She was something of a spiritual role-model for me, with her clear-cut unworldliness, her spiritual gifts, her patent love for the Lord and commitment to His call.

She has recorded in this book, the story of her call and ministry in India, and the events leading up to that ministry. She writes with candor and simplicity. There is adventure, hazard, and courage in her narrative, and throughout an acknowledgment of dependency on God. This narrative is factual and exciting, and I recommend it to you. We will all be the better for reading it.

Aubrey T. Phillips
Blairsville, Georgia

Introduction

I joyfully present this book to the world as a testimony of what our heavenly Father can and will do in guiding a life through difficult circumstances.

He Who makes the impossible possible never fails those who dare to step out upon His promises with faith and obedience to work in the interest of His Kingdom. My reason for writing is to encourage everyone who reads this to completely surrender to His Divine Will. Stand upon His Word and doubt not when facing the "Red Seas" along the way. Obey the word God gave to Moses for the children of Israel to "Go Forward." There will always be victory on the other side.

And when he putteth forth his own sheep, he goeth before them, and the sheep follow him: for they know his voice.

John 10:4

Chapter 1
Preparation

If a man therefore purge himself from these, he shall be
a vessel unto honour, sanctified, and meet for the master's
use, and prepared unto every good work.

2 Timothy 2:21

An impelling consciousness of God has been prevalent in my life since the early age of nine years. In
a small Baptist church located in north Georgia, I was
aware of hearing the voice of the Lord for the first time
in my life. I answered the call to kneel at an altar of
prayer and felt His divine touch upon a child's heart.
From that moment, the genesis of a divine communion
between my spirit and that of the heavenly Father
became evident. The life that God required of me during
childhood and young adult years was so different from
those around me, that I was often puzzled and per-
plexed. Later I realized that it was nothing other than
His divine protection to preserve and prepare me for the
Master's service.

The enemy tried to take my life at the age of ten
years by afflicting me with a severe case of diphtheria.
A high risk procedure was performed and through the
intervention of God, my life was spared and I was
healed. This was one of many incidents that the Lord
used to train me for a life of travel, sacrifice and service
for Him. Often I was sent forth, even as a child, from the

comforting arms of Mother, suitcase in hand, for weeks, or even months, to serve others in need. An invalid grandmother, who required constant care and attention, was placed in my charge when I was only ten years of age. For five years, my life was devoted to her care and safekeeping. My mother once remarked, "Pearl, it seems that you, amongst all of my children, are the one who is required to leave me most frequently to help someone else." Yet, through the heartaches of assuming adult responsibilities while being only a child, I see nothing but preparation for a life of service to a deserving God. These experiences are not remembered with regret, but rather, are considered to be stepping stones toward a sacrificial and abundantly blessed life.

At the age of thirteen, in the same small Baptist church where I first became conscious of that higher power, I again felt the Father's touch, but this time through a glorious experience of conversion. The same night, He also called me to a ministry of soul-winning. Immediately I began my task of winning souls by persuading some of my friends to also accept the Lord Jesus in that very service. This divine call of soul-winning has never left me; however, there was a period of time during which I did not fully understand all that the call meant. I know now for sure, that these too were years of preparation.

After several years away from home at boarding school and in training, I taught elementary school, but soon learned that this was not to be my vocation. The intense hunger for a deeper and closer walk with God increased until one night in December, 1931, it was climaxed by a heavenly visitation such as I had never known. The Lord gloriously filled me with His Holy Spirit, at which time I gladly and joyfully yielded my life completely and wholly to His cause. At that moment the purifying and cleansing rain of heaven flooded my heart and soul, causing me to surrender all — my ambition, my teaching career, my friends, everything to the Lord. I promised to go wherever He sent me. There are many things I do not know and never expect to know in this life, but I know the joy of a full surrender to God. Paul said, *"But what things were gain to me, those I counted loss for Christ" (Philippians 3:7).* Amen!

From the glorious night of my infilling, I could not pursue my career as a teacher with ease and contentment because of the inward urge to work in God's vineyard. Finally, the dealings of the Lord became so intense that I determined to enter full time ministry for God regardless of the cost. Since it was during the depression, money was very scarce. When the final decision of obedience was reached, and the resignation from my position was offered, I had the sum of fifty cents in cash, and one dress that was suitable to wear in the pulpit.

The day following my resignation, a most wonderful experience occurred, which confirmed the step I was taking. In the morning service during worship hour, I received a special anointing from the Holy Spirit. It seemed as though I had been transformed by the Spirit, and the Lord spoke clearly and definitely in words of prophecy saying, "You will cross the sea."

Four and one-half years of ministry in America followed, during which the Lord confirmed His Word with signs following according to Mark 16:20. *"And they went forth, and preached every where, the Lord working with them, and confirming the word with signs following."*

Again and again the call to "cross the sea" was confirmed and I knew assuredly that India was to be the land of my adoption. God has His own way of reminding us of our failures in obedience, so He revealed to

3

another person that "NOW" was the time to leave for the foreign field. Although never doubting my eventual departure for India, I was making no preparation for this ministry. My appetite had begun to diminish and consequently, my body began to grow weak and my health fail. This naturally alarmed me and I sought deliverance through requesting prayer of the church elders. One of the ministers who prayed for my healing obeyed the Holy Spirit's revelation and said to me, "Pearl, when you obey your call to India, your health will be restored." That, for me, was the "Go!" signal.

Chapter 2
Separation

And every one that hath forsaken houses, or brethren, or sisters, or father, or mother, or wife, or children, or lands, for my name's sake, shall receive an hundredfold, and shall inherit everlasting life.

Matthew 19:29

Preparations for my departure to India involved thousands of miles of arduous travel across the nation. In addition to the time spent following a busy ministry itinerary, many tedious hours were spent in obtaining my passport and visa, being inoculated against various tropical diseases, booking passage, and attending to all the minute details involved in foreign travel. Yet finally, and inevitably, the day came when my reservations were made on the *S.S. President Wilson*. I would be sailing from San Francisco on March 27, 1936.

Three months prior to my departure, while riding along the highway on the way to a church service, the Lord made it known to me that the time of my departure was not to be immediate. I remarked to my traveling companion, "Somehow I feel I will not be going to India just yet." For many months I had carried a tremendous burden for the teeming millions in the spiritually dark land of India who were steeped in sin, superstition, and bondages of heathen religion. Suddenly the burden lifted and it was gone! There was nothing but a void in my

5

soul and I wept bitterly. When we arrived at the church, I received a letter indicating that my permit to India had not yet been approved, and there would be a three month delay.

During those three months, however, the Lord opened doors for ministry in America and many souls found Christ and were blessed by the visitation of His presence. So, although I had suffered a gross disappointment because of the three month delay, I later learned it was part of the plan of my Heavenly Father to reveal His power in guiding a life. I found that our faith always has to be tried, *"That the trial of your faith, being much more precious than of gold that perisheth, though it be tried with fire, might be found unto praise and honour and glory..." (1 Peter 1:7).*

Time passed quickly during those days of waiting and itinerating, and yes, soon the day arrived when I was faced with saying good-bye to those things dearest to me — home, friends, mother, dad, family — all that a young woman cherishes most. The day before my train trip to San Francisco, the last farewell service was given in Toccoa, Georgia, near my home. Many close friends and relatives gathered to say good-bye.

Although this was a very sad occasion, and I wept much, my heart held a rainbow of promises. Heaven's sunshine flood cast such glory rays of happiness, that I could only smile in my soul through the torrents of tears which wet my face. The joy that comes from following Jesus far exceeds one's greatest expectations and causes this life's heartaches to diminish quickly and take refuge behind the shadow of His promise. The safest place in all this world is the place of duty for God's wings are over it, and God's peace guards it!

The next morning found me boarding the train in Toccoa, Georgia, at 4:00 a.m. for San Francisco, over 3,000 miles away. Rev. Andrew Cauthen Craft, a leader in the early days of the Pentecostal movement in the South, brought me to the station. In my early Christian life and ministry, he was a great blessing to me. In meetings and conferences, he frequently gave me opportunities to speak, for he knew about my call to India. He did everything he could to encourage me.

It was also in his home that I received my vision of heaven and hell, which is written in another book that has been in circulation for decades. This account of the supernatural has been and continues to be a blessing to many even to this day.

When I was preparing for my journey, I stayed in the Craft home for a while. He gave me, as he would to his own daughter, little articles I valued highly on the mission field. During this "packing" period, he came to me several times and placed money in my hands saying, "Sister Pearl, I want you to use this for your food along the way. I want you to have plenty."

As he was saying his farewell at the train station, he remarked, "I may not be here when you come back, but I will meet you up yonder." His words turned out to be just as he said, for he passed away a few weeks before I returned home. Indeed, I shall greet him again on the other side some day.

While most of the world quietly slept, I had embarked upon a journey that would change the course of my entire life, for at last I had stepped out on my Father's divine promises and had literally answered the call to "cross the sea." In the darkness of the early morning, the train left the station and gradually gained speed to match that of my own heart's racing. However, it was just moments before I would feel the first test of my soul's consecration.

As I looked out the window while the train passed nearby the place most dear to me — home — I felt pangs of this testing. Was it really worth it all to give up those who I loved for those who I did not even know? Were the heart-rending agonies of the so recent farewells worth traveling thousands of miles and enduring many hardships just to greet a new way of life and those bound in a heathen land? These fleeting thoughts left when I found myself looking up into the face of my loving Heavenly Father and I needed no further reassurance. Yes, my consecration stood fast! For Him, I would give up life itself!

With great joy in my heart, overwhelming and far surpassing the natural desires for what I had just left behind, I looked ahead to the life chosen for me by the Lord Himself and knew that the consecration surely still held fast. The answer was still "Go!"

As we swiftly sped westward through the cool, lovely lowlands, the majestic Rocky Mountains, and the vast expanses of the still desert, all God's own creation, His mellowing presence guided my happy heart through the day and closer to the actual point of embarkation, the city of San Francisco. His blessings were so very real and His presence so abiding during the three day journey, that I knew for a surety, that this was the prelude to a most wonderful voyage.

I had only one night and a few hours the next morning to spend in San Francisco, during which I did a bit of last minute shopping. At about 1:00 p.m., on March 27, 1936, I went on board the *S.S. President Wilson,* one of the lovely "President" ocean liners.

When I reached my cabin, I closed the door and knelt to pray. I asked the Lord to give me a traveling companion with whom I could pray while on the high seas, and He answered immediately. I had started to the upper deck to see the ship embark, and on the way I met a dear missionary lady from Alabama. She was all that I could wish for, and was on her fourth trip to China. She came from my beloved Southland.

Hundreds of people swarmed the docks, relatives and friends of the many passengers on board. A colorful snowfall of confetti suddenly enveloped us as the passengers on deck were now joined to their loved ones only by brightly colored paper streamers tossed to the throngs of well-wishers below. They were beautiful, yet flimsy strands that soon were to be broken.

There were no visible streamers to connect me with the loved ones I was leaving behind, since none were there to see me off. Nevertheless, I could feel the cords of love that bound me fast to thousands of true friends whose prayers would follow me across the briny deep. Their prayers would continue to strengthen me as I labored for the Master in the land of my adoption.

It was an exciting moment for all when the ship began to slowly move from the docks. The space between us and the land we loved widened ever so gradually until we were out to sea. What a feeling of adventure swept over me as the ship gained speed. The skyline of the city became dim and finally faded away.

The last rays of the evening sun cast their reflection on the Golden Gate as we passed through, and then I went to my cabin to begin a new life.

Chapter 3
Aloha!

For we know that if our earthly house of this tabernacle were dissolved, we have a building of God, an house not made with hands, eternal in the heavens. For in this we groan, earnestly desiring to be clothed upon with our house which is from heaven.

2 Corinthians 5:1,2

I soon learned that there were several missionaries among the passengers and life did not become monotonous, even though we were on the ocean for a total of five weeks. There were prayer meetings and worship services all along, besides the daily prayer times I had with the friend the Lord gave me.

It took one week to reach Hawaii, and we were happy to be able to go ashore — to stand again on solid ground. In the early morning of April 3, I went on deck to get my first glimpse of Honolulu. While yet a good distance from port, I could see Diamond Head, its famous mountain, as we entered the harbor. As the ship moved slowly in, I could get a clearer view of the island, which looked so fresh and full of life and color, lying out before me. As the ship drew nearer, I could sight the stately palms, and then people walking along the pier. The pilot came on board and we soon pulled into port. Natives began to dive for coins, and the band started playing welcome songs in the exotic native Hawaiian style, the most famous one being, "Aloha", the welcome song of the island. The gang plank was placed, and there were merry hearts as loved ones greeted each other.

After breakfast, my friend and I left the boat and started across the island to see its many lovely sights. Flower girls met us at the entrance with beautiful leis of exotic flowers to wear. We watched them make the leis and they gave us some of the flowers which were being used. A woman guide then took us to see the almost perpendicular 1,200 foot cliff, Pali, which is an historical landmark on the island.

From Pali, we went to the Punch Bowl, which is the crater of an extinct volcano. We could stand on the monument in the center of the mound and see every port in Hawaii. Arrows bearing names of important places pointed in the direction of their location, so we were able to get an idea of what we were seeing. We saw the naval base at Pearl Harbor, and other islands offering many places of interest. We were escorted by our guide through the heart of the city to Waikiki Beach. It was indescribable beauty. Such lovely grandeur and breathtaking color! Honolulu was a burst of flame — gold, yellow, lavender, pink, red, and every color one could imagine. Each street lined from beginning to end with massive blossom covered trees, was separated by color. I remember one looked as if it were covered with wisteria vine, but it was "just a tree" full of flowers. There were coconuts, pineapple, and other fruits growing along the streets, which added beauty to the scene.

Our tour brought us to the famous Royal Hawaiian Hotel, where we meandered through its lovely grounds. As we sat down to rest in comfortable plush chairs, we were reminded of what heaven will be; all that is beauty and then more, for it will be perfect! We will never be separated, but will spend eternity with those we love and with whom we have enjoyed pleasant associations. Inside those pearly gates is joy forever. How marvelous! I opened my Bible and read 2 Corinthians 5:1,2.

> For we know that if our earthly house of this tabernacle were dissolved, we have a building of God, an house not made with hands, eternal in the heavens. For in this we groan, earnestly desiring to be clothed upon with our house which is from heaven.

This portion of the Word seemed so fitting as I sat beholding God's glorious creation.

Chapter 4
Lost and Found

But if our gospel be hid, it is hid to them that are lost: In whom the god of this world hath blinded the minds of them which believe not, lest the light of the glorious gospel of Christ, who is the image of God, should shine unto them.

2 Corinthians 4:3,4

My gratitude and intense appreciation for being allowed to absorb such breathtaking beauty as lovely Hawaii afforded was great, but soon I found myself, with my fellow passengers, sailing eastward again. Our next stop was to be Kobe, Japan.

The voyage between Hawaii and Japan was most interesting. We ran into a typhoon, which is common in those waters, and I saw the waves wash the upper deck of our ship. In fact, I remained on deck during the storm and watched it, for I felt that God was in the midst of it all, showing forth His power. A deck steward passed by and saw me sitting there near where the waves were lashing the deck, and he exclaimed, "Lady, if you can remain on the upper deck during a storm such as this, you are a good sailor!" His chance remark proved to me, as well as to the adversary, that Jesus had delivered me from the sea sickness which had troubled me slightly at the beginning of the voyage.

A source of great entertainment were the flying fish which performed for us as though on a perfectly timed schedule. They seemed to be trained by the Master Trainer Himself to entertain pilgrims on the high seas. The fish would rise in schools and soar very gracefully through the air for a long distance, with their bodies glistening in the bright sunlight. What an unforgettable sight! The Lord is so thoughtful of His children that He leaves nothing off the program that would make them happy, when He sends them forth to harvest.

And when he putteth forth his own sheep, he goeth before them....

John 10:4a

Upon reaching Japan, I had my first glimpse of the Far East and it was an experience I shall never forget. It was April and cherry blossom time in Japan. Everyone seemed cheerful and excited but my heart was made sad as I saw trusting souls climbing the hills to worship at the shrines of idol gods. I desperately longed to tell them of the One who came to set men free and give them Life, but I could not speak their language. The language barrier is a great divider, and has been since the time of the confusing of tongues at the Tower of Babel.

My friend and I decided we would take a train trip to Kyoto, but we boarded the wrong train in that ultramodern station. Many trains were departing in different directions, and we found ourselves in a small station in Kyoto where no one spoke English. It was a strange and lonely feeling to be stranded where no one could help us. In answer to whispered prayer, we suddenly saw a woman coming toward us who turned out to be German. She very graciously called a taxi for us and directed the driver to take us to the main station where someone could speak and understand our language.

Many are stranded today in this world who do not understand the language of our Lord, and they so desperately need someone to show them the way. Those who direct others in a strange land are required to know not only the language of the foreigner, but the language of the country in which they are located. So it is with one who points souls to the Lamb of God. He must know the need of the lost one and also be able to commune with the One who can supply that need.

...he which converteth the sinner from the error of his way shall save a soul from death, and shall hide a multitude of sins.

James 5:20b

Chapter 5
Begging, Begging, Begging,

The Spirit of the Lord is upon me, because he hath anointed me to preach the gospel to the poor; he hath sent me to heal the brokenhearted, to preach deliverance to the captives, and recovering of sight to the blind, to set at liberty them that are bruised, to preach the acceptable year of the Lord.

Luke 4:18,19

After an unforgettable introduction to the exotic Far East, my curiosity mounted to an almost insatiable peak as I anxiously awaited the sight of Shanghai, China. I had not long to wait, for Shanghai was only a few days run from Kobe. The city is situated on a small river, the Woosung, about twelve miles from its mouth.

The thick darkness of night blanketed Shanghai as the ship dropped anchor on the nineteenth of April. I was later informed that we were forced to anchor in midstream because of low tide some distance from shore. On board ship one usually sleeps quite soundly, for the lulling movement of the ship and the clear atmosphere at sea are conducive to deep slumber, so I did not awaken until morning. Upon awakening, I realized the ship was not moving, so I stood on my bunk and peered through the porthole in an effort to see where we were. In these early morning hours of April 20, to my astonishment, I beheld a sight familiar to Shanghai and her unbe-

19

lievably poor mode of river life. It was a heart-stirring experience, the impact of which was so strong, that its most minute details were indelibly stamped upon my memory.

The city proper was extremely filthy, so much so, that only foreigners with much stamina and fortitude could endure its stench. River life afforded even less attraction, and I was made to wonder how the Chinese lived, thrived, and multiplied in the midst of such disease and death. Thousands of these people lived on the water in boats called sampans, and realized their livelihood from the water. They were born, lived and died, without having the privilege of a home as we know it, and endured hardships of unheard-of-poverty.

As I gazed through my porthole upon this astounding scene of destitute degradation, strange sounds wafted upward to my ears. Several shrill voices were crying in broken English, "Mon-ey, mon-ey." What then met my gaze would have melted the heart of the most hardened. A sampan had been rowed alongside our ship by its women occupants, whose duty it was to ply the oars. I saw an entire family of Chinese, from youngest to eldest, begging for money. They were extending long poles with mesh bags attached to the ends, to the passengers who stood on deck. The passengers were dropping small coins into the bags. I then saw the begging and starving Chinese carefully place their poles and nets under the ship's drain in order to catch a new supply of sustenance — the stream of garbage which issued from the ship's kitchen. The most touching sight of all was the outreach of a baby's bony hand as he grabbed vegetable scraps from the flow of refuse and began to hungrily devour them. The whole family joined in the feast and my own appetite disappeared as my heart sank heavily. My soul cried through a breaking voice, "Lord, I cannot bear this. If India is like this, how can I endure the pain that it brings to my heart?" Yet I had much more to see before I left China.

On going ashore, I immediately found that I would not be inclined to linger amid the novel sights, for the sundry stenches which permeated the air could not be called enticing. Although the arresting sights of Shanghai, its striking Oriental costumed inhabitants, and quaint out-of-the-way curio shops provided a form of new attraction, I was not prepared to plow my way through the exceedingly filthy and narrow streets to meet with them again.

Poverty stricken beggars swarmed me, crowding so close that they touched me, begging, begging, begging. Mothers, slight of build and thin, with emaciated babies in their arms, ran after me, only to be outrun by the *coolie* who pulled my rickshaw out of their reach.

In the more affluent section of the city, I remember the beautiful silver, fragile china, rare lace, ivory and jade. I saw lovely carved chests of teakwood and admired rich cloth from many lands as they were displayed in the city's huge stores. Nevertheless, the thing I remembered most vividly through the years is the vast horde of beggars with their unending chant, the heart's plea for daily bread. I later found India's poverty equaled and even exceeded that of China's, and so for six years, I was not able to escape the squalid scene.

Great consolation comes through the Scriptures, for we may read in the fourth chapter of Luke's writing the words of Isaiah, *"The Spirit of the Lord is upon me, because he hath anointed me to preach the gospel to the poor...."* The King of the universe, the Lord God Almighty, Heaven's Gift to Earth, loves the poorest of the poor and offers the same benefits of this so glorious Spirit-filled walk to the most destitute as well as to the richest. He is our able God, the tempest-calming Master, Who knows no defeat!

Hong Kong, 813 miles away, was our next stop. We were in port only for a few hours. This time was spent admiring the natural beauties of the terrain. Hong Kong is an island of lofty peaks and there is scarcely a level acre on the whole island. Views from the peaks afford a magnificent panorama of the surrounding countryside, the town below, the harbor along which the city is built, and the blue expanse of seemingly never-ending water.

I spent some time shopping, and purchased an exquisite carved teakwood chest at an unbelievably low price. I also enjoyed a short visit with some missionaries who were stationed there, and had an interesting lesson in the art of eating rice with chopsticks.

When we sailed from this port, on April 25, 1936, it was our privilege to have a very distinguished person aboard — Dr. Mary Stone. She was the first Chinese woman not to have had bound feet. The cultivation of small feet was one of many Chinese customs still prevalent at that time. It was regarded by the higher classes as a mark of distinction. In conforming to the ritual, the feet of all females were closely bandaged during infancy and early childhood. Dr. Stone, having Christian parents, was spared the painful and crippling ordeal. Through her Christian heritage and a personal knowledge of Jesus Christ as Savior, she later became a missionary to her own people.

Chapter 6
In India at Last, and Happy

Behold, we count them happy which endure....

James 5:11a

The 626 miles from Hong Kong to Manila were quickly covered and on the third day from Hong Kong, we reached Manila. I shall never forget my impressions when I saw "Old Glory" flying on the island. Before I realized what was happening, tears were flowing down my face in profusion. That was the first time I had seen the American flag since I left my beloved homeland. After viewing a few cities in the East, I was very acutely aware of the meaning of that flag. How keenly we become aware of our God-given heritage when it suddenly slips away. Every young man and boy in Manila seemed to have one common ambition, to visit the U.S.A.

My trips ashore afforded an interesting pastime. I joined a group of sightseers and journeyed into the villages to view the life of the natives. We saw the 100 year old church with its bamboo pipe organ, and other sights of interest. We made a trip to the old city of Manila in a *carretta*, a horse-drawn carriage. In the villages, we watched the art of handcraft in operation, and purchased some unique baskets native to the island. The Filipinos were happy to show us their little houses built on stilts several feet above the ground. They were made of bam-

23

boo, with spaces between each strip in the floor so wide that one could see the ground below. There was no furniture and only the barest necessities in the little doll-like houses. I wondered how they could exist under such seemingly primitive circumstances, but climate and customs blend together in each country to produce conditions suitable to its inhabitants.

Cruising along between the islands and the mainland from Manila to Singapore, we experienced one of the most thrilling legs of our voyage. Often we could see the islands, some of which reached out to the Philippines and Indonesia.

Singapore was an English colony at that time and its name means "a place of lions." This was a strange name for the city because I was informed that lions had never been known there. Tigers, which once abounded, were occasionally encountered, much to the alarm of the population since they were reputed to have eaten an average of one man a day. Some of Singapore's chief attractions were its near perfect climate and the convenience of travel communication. Steamships passing eastward or westward, from whatever ports, visited this touching point. I decided to change ships in Singapore and take a British-India vessel to Calcutta to save the long trip by train through India's intense heat in May.

On board the *S.S. Shirala*, I contracted a tropical fever called *dinghu*, which resulted in severe illness. I refused medical attention, though hundreds had fallen victim to this dreaded disease on that ship. I was urged by many to take capsules and other medicinal aids. I told them I wished to trust the Lord for my deliverance, for He had healed my body many times before. There was no one who could pray the prayer of faith for me, so I grew steadily worse by the hour. I had never experienced such pain. Every joint felt as though it was being pulled apart and my head ached with sickening pain. My temperature rose higher and higher until I was very restless and miserable. I knew that each grinding of the motors took me farther and farther away from home and loved ones. What would they say if they knew of my condition? If my parents were aware of the fact that their daughter was seriously ill on the high seas half way around the world, they would be very troubled, but they would pray. I am sure someone prayed, because on the second night of my illness the Lord spoke to me.

The American evangelist's wife, Mrs. Dunlop, who was also headed for India with her husband and changed ships with me in Singapore, had left me to go to dinner and I was alone with the Lord. Clearly and distinctly, these words came, "Sing!"

I answered, "Lord, how can I sing?" The third time the command was more urgent and I found myself singing the little chorus:

"It takes the storm clouds to form the rainbow;

It takes the night time to show the stars;

It takes the crushing to bring forth fragrance,

And make eternal life's withering flowers;

It takes the furnace the gold to brighten;

The sculptor's chisel with blow on blow;

The marble shaft in such polished beauty;

So trials make God's love to glow."

It seemed that an unseen force took possession of my vocal organs and sang that chorus through them. Of course, that was the Holy Spirit, who was guiding and directing me on this mission. Praise the Lord! What a joy to have such assistance! By the time the last word was sung, all my pain and fever were gone and I was healed. My friend rejoiced with me when she returned from the dining room and found me sitting up — well!

The day after my healing we arrived at Rangoon, Burma. I had a chance to go on deck and gave witness to what my wonderful Lord — the Great Physician — had done for me. I did not go ashore, however, for we were anchored in midstream, quite a distance from the shore. I could see the pagodas and was reminded of some of Adoniram Judson's bitter pioneer missionary experiences in Rangoon, when he was blazing a trail for evangelism in that dark land. I realized that my recent trial was mild compared to what he endured for the sake of Christ.

In a few days I was watching the changing scenes along the Hoogly River as the *S.S. Shirala* moved slowly toward Calcutta. The scenery was beautiful to behold and my heart was filled with joy and expectation at the thought of being so near the land of my adoption. Many thoughts were chasing each other through my mind and I frankly admit that I was excited, to say the least.

Soon we pulled into port at Kidapoor Docks at 10:45 a.m., May 15, 1936. Being already on deck, I soon saw a young American woman standing on the pier. It was Miss Effie Barker, who had come to meet me. With her was Rev. Sneed of the Brethren Mission, who had come along to help get my luggage through customs. When the gang plank was set up, scores of dark-skinned porters ran up to the cabins and began to load our luggage on their heads. I used the word *jah*, meaning "go", but it had no effect whatsoever. There was a real scramble as a dozen men grabbed luggage from one another, each one determined that he was going to get the haul. Finally, Effie arrived and straightened them out.

In a matter of minutes we had gone through customs and had all my possessions onto a cart which was pushed by two men through the streets. We went by horse cart to the railroad station. After doing a bit of shopping, we took the evening train for Jasidih Junction, where I was to be stationed. It was a strange looking train to me, quite different from what I was used to in America. We slept on shelves without much padding on them, or at least we reclined as the train jolted and rocked along through the night. It was still dark when we reached our destination. When we arrived at the station, Effie called an open taxi. She said, "We take a taxi tonight, but after this it will be an oxcart."

On our way to the mission station, I saw many people sleeping on the ground with their feet almost in the road. This all seemed strange to me, but before long I, too, was sleeping outside because of the heat. The Lord provided a bamboo cot for me and I felt very grateful to be elevated a little above the ground, since there were so many moving things like snakes, lizards, and scorpions crawling around at night. This was the beginning of six years of labor in India and I was thankful every day that I was privileged to be there.

Chapter 7
A New World

The name of the Lord is a strong tower: the righteous runneth into it, and is safe.

Proverbs 18:10

Pentecostal Holiness Mission Station
Jasidih Junction, Bihar, India

On my first morning in India, May 16, 1936, I was awakened by a very familiar sound. A black crow, perched on the outside shutter of the window near my bed, was joyfully singing, "Caw, caw, caw." I had heard that sound all my life in the foothills of the Blue Ridge Mountains of north Georgia where my family lived. Did my Heavenly Father send that crow to greet me in order to make me feel at home in a strange land? I wouldn't put it past Him, for He is always mindful of His children who obey Him. Praise His Name!

The crow didn't seem to blend in with the white-washed walls with gray lizards crawling on them. I learned later that it was a common inhabitant of India. God loves all His little creatures and places them wherever He chooses.

The earth is the Lord's, and the fulness thereof; the world, and they that dwell therein.

Psalm 24:1

There were many strange flying and crawling things — some dangerous, but many were harmless. It

29

took me a while to learn the difference. Hordes of flies and mosquitoes were forever a problem. With no screens on the doors and windows, most anything could come in when they were open. Sometimes, when I was studying my lesson by the window at night, a big beetle would fly in and hit me in the head. I had to use a net canopy over my bed at night to protect me from the mosquitoes. Even stinging scorpions and poisonous snakes made their way into my room at times, but the Lord protected me. It was indeed a new world and I knew I had much to learn. Most important, however, was the assurance that I was where the Lord wanted me to be.

About the first thing a missionary has to consider upon arriving in a foreign country is learning the native language. Interpreters may be used, but being able to speak the language of the people is far more effective. Therefore, it was arranged for me to begin studying the Hindi language with a native teacher an hour a day, except on Sunday. Because of an experience I had in America shortly after the Lord called me to India, I thought perhaps He would give me their language supernaturally.

This experience happened in a church in Georgia one Sunday morning where I had been invited to minister. As I was ready to take the last step onto the platform, the Lord stopped me. Suddenly in a vision, I was in India, standing before a group of natives. I preached the Word of God to them in what I learned later was the Hindi language. Seven of them accepted the Lord as their Savior. They prayed with their faces on folded hands touching the floor, which I didn't know was their manner of praying until that time. I do not know how long the vision lasted. The congregation sat quietly in the church until the Lord released me. When I told them what had happened, the Spirit of the Lord took over and we had a time of great rejoicing, salvation and deliverances. How great is our God! When I reached India, I heard some of the words I spoke in the vision, and also recognized them as I studied the Hindi language.

One night I even dreamed a full sentence. The next morning I rattled off a string of words and asked Effie if they meant anything. She informed me that it was a complete sentence, but I had not yet started studying the language.

While studying, I was able to begin using my newly acquired words in the villages as I accompanied Effie when she went to teach the people. We sang choruses in Hindi before she spoke. That was a joy to me. Evangelistic work was my calling and I was happy for any opportunity to fulfill it. That didn't last long, however, because there came about a change in my situation.

When I first arrived at Jasidih, Effie was the only missionary there. The Superintendent of the Pentecostal Holiness work in India, Rev. Jack Turner, his wife Olivia, and their five children were in the mountains in Darjeeling. Since all schools for American children were in the mountains, they lived there during the season while their four older children were in school. In November of 1936, I was asked to look after the children while their parents, along with their youngest son, came down to Jasidih to welcome some of their missionaries arriving from America at that time.

While in Darjeeling, I continued my language study with a new teacher. At the end of the school season, the children and I returned to home base in Jasidih to find a new arrangement at the mission station. The Turner family was occupying their own home where I stayed with Effie when I first arrived. Rev. Marvin Parrish, his wife Alma, and their two little girls, Marguerite and Helen, now lived in the larger house, which formerly was used for Effie's orphanage. In addition, four of us who were single missionaries, Effie Barker, Emma Yeatts, Emma Brittain, and I were each given a room in the same house as the Parrish family. We were a big happy family. Praise the Lord! I was not a member of the Pentecostal Holiness organization, but they were kind to let me stay there until the Lord placed me where He wanted me to work.

In March of 1937, I went to Landour, Mussourie, in the Hemalaya Mountains, to attend language school, where I stayed in the Assembly of God Rest Home. My private teacher was filled with the Holy Spirit. It was a joy to study the Bible in Hindi with a Christian native teacher. He came at six o'clock in the morning and we had my lesson out on the lawn. My little room was outside the main building. It was built on top of some *go downs* (storage rooms) on the level below. I usually had time to take a nap before breakfast after the teacher left.

One morning I read a portion of Scripture, either a miracle or a parable, with my teacher. I read it again and then I went into the house and took my nap. When I woke up, I wrote it correctly from memory. That is one of the ways I recognized the work of the Holy Spirit in my study of the language. Even though I was not given the language supernaturally, the Lord helped me in many ways to learn what I learned. Blessed be His Name! It is not that He was not able to give me the language, but rather, that He is all-sufficient for these things. The Scripture is filled to overflowing with accounts of His all-sufficiency.

I finished my first year of Hindi and returned to Jasidih to continue language study with a private teacher. I had learned enough to get around and do a bit of preaching. I expected to return to Landour the next year for my second course, but the Lord had other plans.

Trust in the Lord with all thine heart; and lean not unto thine own understanding. In all thy ways acknowledge him, and he shall direct thy paths.

Proverbs 3:5,6

Chapter 8
Deliverance From Robbers

The angel of the Lord encampeth round about them that fear him, and delivereth them.

Psalm 34:7

In February of 1938, there was a gruesome robbery in the home of an Indian family next door to the mission station in Jasidih. A gang of 24 men dressed in *saffron*, "holy men" robes came to their door, rushed in and began snatching the gold jewelry from the women's necks, ears, and wrists. The women, with their skin torn and bleeding, were screaming. The man of the house tried to protect his family and the robbers knocked him down. Some of the men at the mission heard the noise and ran to help them. No one was seriously injured but the wealth of the family was gone. It is said that the Indians preserve their wealth in jewelry on their women.

On the heels of this event, I was invited to go to Kanpur by a missionary friend, Madeline Cousins, that I had met at Landour. She wanted me to come for some prayer ministry. Several of the missionaries accompanied me to the train station to see me off. Emma Yeatts handed me a slip of paper with this verse of Scripture on it, *"Fear thou not; for I am with thee: be not dismayed; for I am thy God: I will strengthen thee; yea, I will help thee; yea, I will uphold thee with the right hand of my righteousness" (Isaiah 41:10).* That was a great comfort to me as

I traveled alone all night until the late afternoon of the next day.

It seemed that all concerned had a spirit of apprehension as I boarded the train. Even the British breakman came to my door and said, "Lady, don't fear. If you need help, I am two doors down from you." As the train began to gather speed, I knelt and called on the Lord. He gave me sweet assurance and I lay down and took a nap.

I will both lay me down in peace, and sleep: for thou, Lord, only makest me dwell in safety.

Psalm 4:8

When I reached my destination, the city seemed dead. The store fronts were boarded up and deserted. No one was there to meet me. I was able to get a taxi and go to the home of Alice Richey, where Madeline was staying. I learned that the city had been in riots and all stores and businesses were closed.

From that first day, I could not pray, read, or even knit. The powers of darkness were so strong that I felt I could not bear the pressure. After two days there was a real breakthrough and my spirit was free.

If the Son therefore shall make you free, ye shall be free indeed.

John 8:36

That very afternoon, Madeline and I were resting on our cots in our little room. It was an enclosed veranda with small windows close to the ceiling. Suddenly, I heard beautiful music and singing. I asked Madeline if she heard it. She didn't, so I realized I was hearing the heavenly choir. Little did I know that the Lord was preparing me for a mighty miracle of deliverance in that very spot.

The angel of the Lord encampeth round about them that fear him, and delivereth them.

Psalm 34:7

It was Valentine's Day, February 14, 1938. Madeline had retired and I was sitting on the side of my cot with my back to the door writing her a poem. Madeline had left the door open for more air. Suddenly, a gun fired at my back and Madeline screamed. "What's happening here?" I wondered. I stood to see a man leaning over her. The drapes on the door were on fire.

Immediately, I thought of the robbery at Jasidih and another one I had read about recently. Naturally, I thought there were others outside, maybe a gang of them. I stepped inside Alice's room. It was the adjoining room next to ours, and the door was at the head of my cot. Alice arose and asked what was happening. I said, "There's a man in the house. Come." By that time she was out of bed and passing me into our room. She faced the robber who was standing in the doorway with the gun pointed at her. He demanded that she hand him my suitcase, which was nearby.

She told him that I was just a missionary and didn't have any money. She then went out through the dressing room and bathroom, and around to the other side of the house where a Christian Indian couple lived. I heard her scream which confirmed the fact that there were more robbers than the one we saw. A man stepped from the shrubbery and grabbed her by the throat. He had a long knife in his hand, which he brandished in her face. Just then the Christian brother opened his door with a gun in his hand. The robber turned on him, but seeing the gun, he dropped the knife and ran. Praise the Lord!

The wicked flee when no man pursueth: but the righteous are bold as a lion.
Proverbs 28:1

On our side of the house, I stopped a moment before going back into our room. I had to touch God. I said, "Lord, will you fail us now?" He reminded me of how He had protected others when they were in great danger. I began to praise Him and the Holy Spirit lifted me into a realm of victory so great, that I felt I could face anything without fear. I picked up my Bible with my left hand and walked out to face the robber who was still standing in the doorway with the gun in his hand. I stood there with the Bible over my heart, speaking the heavenly language. He also ran away.

I heard Alice talking with the friends in the next apartment and I knew she was safe. Madeline said, "Close the door." When I went to close it, I saw a puddle of blood on the floor. The Lord said, "My blood, like a blanket, covers you and they cannot touch you." Hallelujah!

> So shall they fear the name of the Lord from the west, and his glory from the rising of the sun. When the enemy shall come in like a flood, the Spirit of the Lord shall lift up a standard against him.
>
> Isaiah 59:19

We left our room and went around to where Alice had gone. When we stepped inside, I began to shake like a leaf. That precious anointing had lifted and I felt the impact of the shock.

Alice and the Indian brother went to inform the British official of the robbery. He lived nearby and came over to inspect the place. We all viewed the sight together. There were masks and sandals in the shrubbery, and a large sledgehammer lying at the door by the puddle of blood. There was a trail of blood stains from the door to a large tree a few feet away. In our room, Madeline's mosquito net was torn. My bed was full of cinders from the old fashioned gun that the gunman used. *But we were safe!* We thanked the Lord for His divine protection and also for the law. Police were stationed around our house all night. Instead of sleeping, we three ladies sat on a mattress on the floor all night. We read promises from the Bible, praised the Lord and spoke of all His wondrous works. Glory to His Name!

All the next day, there was a constant stream of people who came by to see the sight. Christians, Moslems and Hindus had to admit that God protected us. Our God was exalted.

Surely the wrath of man shall praise thee: the remainder of wrath shalt thou restrain.

Psalm 76:10

The three robbers were captured that night. At the trial, a local doctor testified that all three of them came to his house that night. With gun in hand, the gunman relating a different story demanded him to remove the bullet from the back of the man that was shot. The doctor refused and put them out, locking the door behind them.

They were college men, we learned. They wanted money and what they thought was a gun under Madeline's pillow. It was a small black flashlight, which they took along with her watch. We felt sure they had been watching us through those high glass windows. They also said they wanted to kill us because we were turning Hindus to Christianity. They didn't know how safe we were in Jesus. Hallelujah!

The gunman received a sentence of two years and the other two were sentenced to one year in prison.

Chapter 9
Called To Puri

Commit thy works unto the Lord, and thy thoughts shall be established.

Proverbs 16:3

I n March of 1938, soon after the robbers ordeal, I began to prepare for my return to Landour for my second year of Hindi in language school. I had made reservations for my lodging in the Assembly of God Rest Home, and also for the train trip. On the day I was due to leave, I packed all my luggage on an ox cart and went to the railway station at Jasidih. Low and behold — I was informed that no trains would be running that day. It was a Hindu holiday.

There was nothing for me to do but return to the Mission and wait. I thought the delay must be for some reason unknown to me. I went to prayer in deep travail for hours. I couldn't believe what was happening. The Lord, by the Holy Spirit, was saying, "Go to Puri, on the coast." I didn't know there was such a place. If I had heard of it, it didn't register in my mind. I said, "Lord, I thought I was to work in the Hindi speaking area. What would the other missionaries think if I changed to another area now?" When I thought like that, everything seemed dark. The Lord kept saying, "Puri." He showed me the Juggernaut Temple and much of the scenery, which I recognized when I went there later.

41

This battle continued until I finally yielded to His will and victory came. I knew that was it. I would go to Puri, wherever that was.

I arose from my knees and picked up a map. By the time I had located it, about 300 miles south of Calcutta on the Bay of Bengal, Madeline and Emma came into my room. They had been listening from another room to my conversation with the Lord. Madeline, looking over my shoulder to the map said, "Pearl, do you think it could be Puri?" I answered, "Yes, it is Puri." A right decision always brings peace. Praise the Lord.

Commit thy works unto the Lord, and thy thoughts shall be established.

Proverbs 16:3

Madeline had never before mentioned Puri to me, but then she began to tell me about the place. She said she had been to Puri and told a person in Cuttack, who was interested in Puri, about my ministry. That was news to me. Someone must have been praying. She went on to say that Puri was only twenty-five miles off the main route to where she was going by train, from Calcutta to Berhampur. She told me that if I would go with her, she would escort me to Puri so I could see the place. She had some Christian friends in Cuttack, fifty miles from Puri, where we could spend our first night. I replied, "Madeline, the Lord has told me *where* to go, but He hasn't told me *when*." Madeline waited another week. Every day of that week, the Lord spoke to me in some way — from the Word of God, in a dream, or some other way, that it was time to go. Praise His Name!

Finally, the week passed and it was time to launch out into the unknown. There we stood on the railway platform at Jasidih Junction. All of my luggage was with me. I said to Madeline, "I am going out like Abraham of old, not knowing whither." I felt so happy and free! When we sincerely obey the Lord and fully trust His guidance, He is obligated to take care of the circumstances.

And when he putteth forth his own sheep, he goeth before them, and the sheep follow him: for they know his voice.

John 10:4

After one night with friends in Cuttack, we journeyed on to Puri. Here we were, with all of our belongings, in a strange city with no place to lay our heads. We set out to look for some Christians. The English Baptists had a Mission Home near the bay, but we were told that no missionary had been able to spend more than three months in Puri. The only semblance of any Christian work we could find was a native man who was supposed to have been in charge of the work of the English Baptists in that place. He very kindly showed us a small room of about eight square feet with walls and a roof. The ground was the floor.

Madeline's servant, who was traveling with us, set up our cots and brought in our food basket. We sat down on our cots and she remarked, "If we only had a table."

I answered, "Never mind, the Lord will supply a table." Shortly thereafter, a servant walked in with a table on his head. We looked at each other and smiled.

She said, "Now, if we only had some chairs."

I replied, "The Lord will provide them, too." In walked the servant with two chairs. Glory to God!

But my God shall supply all your need according to his riches in glory by Christ Jesus.

Philippians 4:19

We stayed about two days and looked over the place. There it was — everything the Lord had shown me was there before my eyes. We had one inquirer who came back many times to hear more about Jesus. We went on to Berhampur to Madeline's destination. I kept praying for the Lord to open the door and direct my getting set up in the place He had chosen for me to work.

Shortly thereafter, I learned that a missionary, Ann Morrow, was due to spend a month in the Baptist Mission Home and I was invited to stay with her. That gave me time to find a place to live. The Lord opened the door to the home of a Scottish-Irish couple who were retired photographers. I rented two rooms with a kitchenette until a little three room house became available. Later the Lord provided a fourteen room house which belonged to a petty queen.

The Lord also provided a native preacher and his family, who were happy to live in the servants quarters at the back of the big house. He had been the British and Foreign Bible Society's colporteur, but they were happy to have him work with me. He and his wife received the Holy Spirit Baptism in a great revival the Lord sent as we prayed and ministered the Word. Several others also received. To God be the glory — Great things He has done!

Chapter 10
Living By Faith

Ye are of God, little children, and have overcome them: because greater is he that is in you, than he that is in the world.

1 John 4:4

My work took me to the nearby villages, ministering on the streets to the people and holding Sunday school with the children under the village trees. A servant asked me to come to his village to pray for the sick and I agreed to go. Juanita Boory went with me. In one of the mud huts, I prayed for a woman who had been sick for two weeks and the Lord instantly healed her. She got up and went to work.

The villagers gathered up the sick into one mud hut. I first cautioned them not to do *puja*, but to pray to Jesus because He is the Healer. Having ministered and left, I returned two days later to check up on the people. I found that all had been healed except for two children. I questioned to see if they had worshipped their gods. The parents of these two were the only ones who had done so. I again explained to their mother about Jesus, prayed for the children again and they were healed.

On another occasion a preacher's wife was sick unto death. All of the missionaries prayed and the Word of the Lord came forth that "She shall live." She got up and was instantly healed.

45

The Lord's care and provision for us sometimes came in unusual ways. One day Juanita and I were having goat feet curry and rice for lunch. I went to open a small can of pears and remarked, "I wish we had some oranges." Before I could sit down, a servant from the railroad station arrived with a tray of oranges sent by the train station master's wife.

Another time found Mrs. Linden and Juanita in the prayer room. The cook mistakenly had not been given the menu. Consequently, there was no food to be prepared. After the service, I went to the dining room and opened the door. There stood a servant with a tray of roast duck, baked potatoes, and ripe tomatoes from the train station master's wife.

On another occasion, I had sent a check for exchange to currency and it was misdirected for a few days. As a result, I had only enough money to get a handful of rice. The cook and I didn't want to tell anyone but the Lord. With the little amount of money, the cook purchased the rice. I had two small pieces of Indian bread and two or three potatoes. Dr. Rose, a woman doctor who was staying with us at the time, went out on the veranda to be greeted by a servant bearing fresh vegetables. In a short while, another servant brought fruit. We both went to the door to find a servant bringing us cold custard. Hot stew came in next and we had a feast!

There were many frequent reminders of God's loving care for His children. One time I was preaching on the streets of Puri near the Hindu temple. Hundreds stopped to listen while I preached through an interpreter. When I got to the message of the Cross, the Hindu leaders began to excite the crowds by calling out about their gods. The crowd was becoming hostile and was about to mob me. I prayed and instantly there was silence until I was finished. I walked away as they cleared a path for me. An educated man walked alongside of me. He was trembling and remarked, "I'd give anything in the world to have your kind of faith." I replied, "Sir, it's not my faith, but Jesus' faith. That's why I'm here, to tell you that Jesus loves you."

In another similar situation, I sang a chorus in the native language and the angry mob was diffused of its hostility. In these ways, our Father reminds us of His presence, for in His Word He promises He will never leave us.

These were but a few events that characterized the first six years I spent serving the Lord as a missionary in India. Towards the end of this time, the Lord provided an automobile and trailer that took me on a 500 mile trip filled with astounding trials and miracles from beginning to end. This supernatural voyage is told in detail in a book I wrote entitled, *500 Miles of Miracles in India*.

By this time World War II had broken out, and India was in the midst of the catastrophe. It became necessary for me to arrange for my return back to the United States. This became a difficult and time consuming task because it required secrecy due to wartime restrictions.

Although I had received instructions from my supporting church in the U.S.A. to leave India as soon as possible, and funds were sent for my return fare, the money did not reach me until I arrived in the States. I sold the automobile and trailer that took me on that memorable miraculous trek across 500 miles of danger and used the money to finance my voyage home, which proved to be far more dangerous.

Chapter 11
War!

He that dwelleth in the secret place of the most High shall abide under the shadow of the Almighty.

Psalm 91:1

One night before Juanita and I knew that we would be leaving by ship, we were having dinner in the home of a friend in Asansol with a couple of missionaries who had already booked their reservations on the same ship. During our time of fellowship around the table, one of them gave a message in tongues and for the first, and only time in my life, I was given the interpretation in writing. I hurriedly picked up a scrap of paper and wrote down some wonderful promises that were a great encouragement to all of us on that most dangerous voyage. It went as follows, "Fear not, for I will be with thee. I will bless thee and sustain thee. When thou passeth through the waters, they will not overflow thee, and I shall bring thee to thy desired haven." Praise the Lord!

O the depth of the riches both of the wisdom and knowledge of God! how unsearchable are his judgments, and his ways past finding out!

Romans 11:33

After Juanita and I had finished our packing and clearing out of Asansol, we went up the country a bit nearer to the port of embarkation, which would either be Bombay or Karachi. We had been invited to the home of

49

a missionary friend, which was part of our Father's wonderful arrangements for us.

And when he putteth forth his own sheep, he goeth before them, and the sheep follow him: for they know his voice.

John 10:4

One night we were praying on the top of a flat-roofed house concerning our trip, and I saw in a vision a shining stream of light on the water like one can see behind a ship as he travels in the moonlight. The words came by the Spirit, "From shore to shore." I took that to mean that the Lord would see us through the perilous waters. Praise His Name!

In trying to get all the legal work done that was required of one who was leaving the country, we spent many days walking from office to office. Still lacking the necessary important papers needed, we were told to go to yet another office. We kept praying and doing whatever we could in personal preparation.

Everything concerning our ship sailing from India had to be done in secret. We would receive a notice to be ready to sail on a certain date from Bombay. Then, at about the time for us to go to Bombay, we would get word to be in Karachi, Pakistan by another date. This seesawing continued for some time.

One day, Juanita said, "Pearl, when you and I are ready to go, the ship will sail." Sure enough, a few days later, an Indian gentleman came and gave us our permit to leave India, and immediately we were notified to be at a designated point at a specified date. So we began a most dangerous voyage to the "good *ole* U.S.A."

The ship had been one of America's three largest ocean liners but had been converted into a troop ship. It had taken 8,000 of our military men to India and was bringing back 1,000 evacuees, 500 missionaries and their children.

Our stateroom was designed to accommodate four people but we were told that 29 military men, whose bunks were still intact, had occupied it on the trip over. Eight of us women got along quite well in it.

Since we traveled in blackout, our portholes were sealed leaving only a tiny blue light in our bathroom. However, we spent little time in our room since the weather was unbearably hot. We were more comfortable on deck and spent a good deal of time there.

Before darkness came, we missionaries would assemble on deck each evening for a time of fellowship in song, prayer and praise. There was nothing we could do and no one was in a hurry to leave, so we "bowed not to the shrine of time" and worshipped our wonderful Lord out on the great ocean. Praise the Lord!

Sometimes we stayed on deck until 2:00 a.m. Then we would go down to our staterooms feeling our way through the darkness. I had been living in blackout conditions in Calcutta and Asansol, so it wasn't anything new to me. I read my Bible in my house trailer by a kerosene lantern with a dark cloth draped over me so that not even a tiny ray of light could filter through. In the building where I held service in Asansol, I read the Bible at night by a small flashlight with heavy drapes over all the windows. Since we were only three miles from a military base, survival restrictions were very serious. This had been good training for me and the experience made it easier for me to endure the things we were going through on board ship in war.

We single women signed up to take a raft and leave the lifeboats for the mothers with children in case our ship was hit by a bomb or torpedo. We often had drills on deck instructing us on how to abandon ship and catch onto a life raft. The instructor said that if we should be hit, the ship would sink within five minutes, so we would have to quickly get as far away from it as possible to miss being pulled in by the suction of a sinking ship. He also warned us that it was not easy to leave something solid like the floor of a ship, and throw yourself into a deep ocean to reach for a raft.

All of that sounded fearful, yet I had the assurance that the ship would not sink. The Lord had said that the waters would not overflow us and He would take us through to our desired haven. Hallelujah!

Our life belts were our constant companions. We slept with them beside us, kept them with us in the dining room, on deck, and everywhere we went. When a ship appeared on the horizon, not knowing if it was an enemy ship or not, the sailors who manned the guns would uncover them and turn them toward the vessel until they received the signal that it was a friendly ship. At such a time, we who were on deck would be prepared to put on our life belts. Thank the Lord, we were never hit, but both the Japanese and Germans were trying to sink us. Two ships sank in front of us and one behind us. We even picked up survivors at one point.

One of the survivors was a young man from Louisiana who survived two shipwrecks. His only possessions were the clothes he wore. Unfortunately he also had a problem with alcohol. I was privileged to lead him to the Lord in the prayer of salvation. From that time to the end of the voyage he came to me daily asking for scriptures that he shared with the crew members below deck. Even after we arrived at our destination, he continued to correspond for the next thirty years about the things of the Lord in his life.

One night a flare was dropped in front of us and we turned around. We traveled back to the Bermuda Islands where we remained out in midstream for several days. We were given two planes assigned to comb the waters ahead of us the rest of the way into New York, and a destroyer escort to travel with us which followed close behind.

The day came when we knew we were nearing our destination and would soon be coming into New York harbor. I was standing at the porthole of our stateroom combing my hair. Suddenly I saw something skim the surface of the water. It came from the direction of the destroyer following behind us. Then I saw that our ship was turning in a complete circle, and brownish looking water was boiling up near the ship. I was told later that our destroyer was sounding depth charges to intercept a torpedo which the enemy had fired to attack our ship. We were informed that ships were being sunk every day along the Atlantic coast. However, there had been too much prayer on that ship and the Lord had too much precious cargo on it for the enemy to be able to destroy it. The Lord spared us. Praise His Name!

As the gang plank went down and we came ashore at New York harbor, we were met by Red Cross workers who had all kinds of good food waiting for us. The one thing I appreciated most was a glass of cold milk that I knew was clean. It was indeed a blessing to enjoy after six years in India where milk from the villages was diluted with water that was far from being clean even after we boiled it.

After being refreshed with the delicious food, we went through customs and the usual red tape upon entering a country. No one except those who have experienced it can imagine what it was like to return to our great country after living in India for six years. I suppose the cleanliness and freshness of everything impressed me more than anything else, along with the abundance of fresh food in the markets and grocery stores. In Puri, India, we could usually get some vegetables and fruit, but sometimes after a Hindu festival, all the shelves were empty in the bazaar and not even a banana could be found. There was one occasion when I couldn't get anything to eat except potatoes for three days, and another time I could only get a starchy Indian vegetable. The Lord enabled me to get away to Calcutta where I could survive. Praise His Name.

In spite of all the hardships and drastic changes in life style, I was very happy in India. I was sent there by the Lord and was never homesick, for I knew I was in His will and nothing else mattered.

It would take several books to tell even the highlights of the happenings of those six years — journeys through dangerous zones, robbers, hurricanes, war, wild animals, snakes, scorpions, and other dangers. On the other side of the coin, there were precious times of fellowship with other missionaries and native Christians; a ministry on the streets of Puri and in villages far and near; and English services on Sundays. The Lord wrought many miracles in answer to prayer and I give Him the glory for six years of fruitful ministry.

Having returned home from India with no funds, I had to look to the Lord for provision for the ministry in America. In answer to prayer, He provided a practically new car and a nice house trailer which I used in traveling through the Southland in revivals, at Bible school for several months, and some pastoral work.

Chapter 12
Back To India

The Lord has done great things for us; whereof we are glad.

Psalm 126:3

During the time since my return to the states, there had been many changes. Some months after I arrived, my father went to be with the Lord. At that time I was in full time evangelistic work, pulling a mobile home from place to place as God opened doors before me. I came off the field for a few weeks during my father's illness and death. Then, since my father was gone, it became my responsibility to look after my mother and teen-age sister, which I was happy to do.

At the close of a great revival in the Full Gospel Church at Fuquay Springs, North Carolina, the leaders asked me to fill in as pastor in place of the one who resigned, until the Lord provided another. I agreed to be there on weekends but continued traveling during the week.

The church provided a house for my mother and sister. I had them moved from Alto, Georgia to Fuquay Springs, where they lived until my sister finished high school.

Since the church leaders were businessmen with a chain of stores, my sister Ruth was blessed with a part-time job in the store at Fuquay Springs, which provided some support for her and my mother. The Lord provided the rest through my ministry.

After Ruth graduated and time was drawing near for my return to India, Ruth and mother wanted to go back to Georgia. One day upon my return from a revival, they asked me what I could do about moving them. We didn't have the money to hire a truck or moving van and I knew there had to be a miracle. I boldly declared that we would pray and God would make a way. While we were on our knees, there was a knock on the door. One of the church brethren had come to tell us that he had to go buy some cattle for his meat market. He was planning to pass through where my mother and sister were going. He would have an empty truck going down, and gladly offered to move them free of charge. Glory to Jesus! That certainly strengthened our faith.

Call unto me, and I will answer thee, and shew thee great and mighty things, which thou knowest not.

Jeremiah 33:3

The Full Gospel Church of Fuquay Springs, North Carolina, invited me to return to India under the sponsorship of their church. That seemed to be God's appointment and I gladly accepted it. They also accepted Juanita, who had returned with me from India in 1942. In addition, Mervin Arnold, who I met at Southeastern Bible School in Atlanta, was also accepted to accompany me as associate in the work in India. Mervin was not a minister, but was very dedicated to the Lord, and proved to be of great help to me on the mission field. I thanked God for both of them and counted it a great honor to have such precious and faithful friends with me.

After weeks of itinerating, the three of us were ready to venture forth on our next missionary journey back to India. At the last minute I sold my car to a minister friend. He and his daughter drove Mervin and me to Chicago, where Juanita was waiting to join us.

We learned from an ad in the newspaper, that passage was available all the way to San Francisco with a young man who was driving there in a Lincoln Continental and needed three passengers. The price was fair, and he was able to take all of our thirteen pieces of small luggage. It was God's provision for His servants and a very pleasant, enjoyable trip across our great country to San Francisco.

We had only one night and part of a day after arriving, during which we did some last minute shopping before boarding our ship, the *S.S. Limburg*, a Norwegian merchant ship. As we were in prayer that night in our hotel room, the Lord gave me a vivid vision of "the great Calcutta killing," which took place about three months after we arrived in India. It was an outburst of rioting between the Hindus and Moslems at the time England was granting home rule to India. Many thousands were slaughtered in different parts of India, but Calcutta seemed to be one of the worst trouble spots.

At the time of this event, Mervin and I were working in Puri, and Juanita was living in Calcutta. She wrote me about some of the horrible things she was seeing from the window of her room. She wrote, "Pearl, the things God showed you in the vision in San Francisco are being enacted before my very eyes."

There was wholesale slaughter on the streets. Cars, buses, and houses were burned. The bodies of men, women, and children were ripped up with bayonets and left on the streets or crammed into manholes to decay. It took months to cleanse the city of the stench of decaying flesh.

There is one note of victory in the story. Only one supposed Christian was known to be killed in the riots, and it was reported that he was a Christian in name only. God took care of His own. Hallelujah!

While on board the *S.S. Limburg* on my way back to India, sailing on the Java Sea, on May 21, 1946, I wrote the following letter to my loved ones back home. It gives some details of the voyage and people aboard ship.

"To the Saints and Friends of the Full Gospel Tabernacle:

Greetings of victory in His love, from the East Indies! It is time I was telling you something about our voyage for we will reach Batavia tomorrow morning and I hope to be able to mail some letters.

To put it in few words, it has been wonderful. The Lord has surely been gracious to us and has given us favor in the eyes of the Officers from the beginning and made them very gracious also. Praise His Name!

They allowed us to have services in the First Class Dining Room each Sunday morning for which we are happy. We were the first to hold religious services on this boat for it is a new one and this is her maiden voyage. The Lord has been with us and the services have been sweet but not many came for most of them were on duty or could not understand English very well. We thank the Lord for those who have come, for some have not missed a time from the beginning. We want you to join us in prayer for those who have attended and also for all we have been privileged to witness to on board. We believe that something has been accomplished for Eternity. Praise the Lord!

There are two other missionaries besides us. One is a lady doctor, Miss Gertrude Smith, who is returning to India to work in a hospital. One doesn't have to be with her long to learn that the medical work doesn't come first with her, for she surely has an experience with God. We have had sweet fellowship with her, also with Mrs. Matthews who belongs to the China Inland Mission and is going to Calcutta to meet her husband. He is in the service, but will soon get his discharge and after visiting his people in Australia, they will return to China to take charge of a mission station there. They were both in China before but were only married in February while he was home on furlough in Canada. She is very dear in the Lord, too. I do not know what one of us would have done on this boat without another missionary, for all the others drink. In the evenings we sing and pray and the others drink and play cards.

Yes, the contrast is great but we realize that we are only trophies of His grace and were it not for that we would be lost, too. Oh, it is so wonderful to know Him. I am so glad I'm numbered with the redeemed ones and I am glad this world is not our home. Hallelujah! We are seeking a City — whose Builder and Maker is God."

It was a rough time for India and for those who were doing missionary work. It was very dangerous to travel and there was robbing and stealing everywhere. Most missionaries were robbed and some lost their lives according to reports we received. Even before we left the ship in Madras on the day of our arrival, a man came on board and told us that a British nurse had been killed on a train the night before and her body thrown out the window. It was the train that left at the same hour we were to leave that night for Calcutta and on the same route. The news was a bit disturbing, but we were looking to God to take care of us. Jesus said, *"And when he putteth forth his own sheep, he goeth before them, and the sheep follow him; for they know his voice" (John 10:4).*

In spite of all the dangers and difficulties, the Lord worked in great ways for two years, even sending a great revival to our mission in Puri. In August of 1947, I wrote the following article in our missionary newsletter entitled, *Mission Echoes From India.*

"Dear Friends in Jesus,

Greetings of praise and victory in His Name.

The Lord has done great things for us; whereof we are glad.
Psalms 126:3

More than a year ago He brought us to this land again to proclaim the Glad Tidings of Great Joy to those who haven't heard and He has wonderfully kept us through these months of bloodshed and anxiety. To Him be praise!

Today we are in a new India. At midnight of August 14th we were awakened by the sound of cannons, the beating of drums, train whistles, bells, etc. Then shouts of victory, and singing as groups passed our bungalow in processions, proclaiming their freedom. The hour of India's Independence has come! We thought of what the Fourth of July means to us and we rejoiced with them, yet, way down deep there was a sob because so many are not really 'free' for they don't know Christ who alone can make men free.

What the future holds for the Christians here we know not but we see His hand in many incidents and realize that He is still brooding over India. Surely there is victory ahead if we are faithful and loyal to Him and true to the heavenly vision. Amen!

During these fourteen and a half months we have seen souls pray through to a real joy in Christ. We have seen the sick healed by His touch, and have had the joy of giving out the Word to many hungry hearts, yet, it seems we have done so little when we look around and see all there is to be done. More than ever we realize that it is, 'not by power, nor by might, but by My Spirit, saith the Lord.' We are learning to lean harder on Him. Praise His Name!

I want to thank each of you for your prayers, also for letters, cards, parcels, tracts, books, love offerings and every expression of love and fellowship. You can never know just what it all has meant to us unless He shows you for there are no words to express it. I say this earnestly. Many times your dollar, or larger amount, has come at a time when we were in a special need and we knew the Lord had sent the needed help through you. I thank Him for those who hear Him and obey. He will repay you an hundredfold. Glory!"

The Lord led me to invite an Indian brother, Jevaratnam, who was mightily used of God for a number of years in India, especially in casting out demons, to come to Puri and minister for a few days. During his stay, we saw him cast out many demons from the village people who came for deliverance. They were changed in minutes from a state of insanity to normal, loving people. Glory to God!

The villages around us were so stirred that the people continued to flow to our mission for prayer day after day, even after the minister left. Some brought chickens, eggs, vegetables, and gifts. We rejoiced to see them blessed and set free by our wonderful Lord. Not that we expected the gifts, but the very desire to give something was a token of their being blessed. The Lord was pouring out His Spirit in our midst and some were receiving great experiences of victory and power. The revival continued on after Mervin and I left.

She and I had spent a whole night in prayer, seeking the Lord for direction, and He definitely spoke to us to go home. Our support had suddenly stopped some months before and we had no word from the church as to an explanation. In a few days after we received the word from the Lord, a letter came from headquarters calling us home. Juanita chose to stay and she took over the work in Puri where the revival continued for some time.

Chapter 13
Shipwrecked in Malta

They that go down to the sea in ships, that do business in great waters; These see the works of the Lord, and his wonders in the deep.

Psalm 107:23,24

Mervin and I were making final preparations for leaving the country from Calcutta where we were staying at the time. One evening a great cloud came over India. Mervin and I were standing outdoors at the place where we were staying. I said to her, "Something terrible has happened in India." I felt a gloom in my soul. We went to a prayer meeting in a home shortly thereafter. Within an hour an automobile passed and from a loud speaker, the announcement came that Mahatma Ghandi, India's notable leader, was assassinated. All India was stirred. He was a Hindu, but was an advocate of peace and loved by many.

We made reservations on a British-India merchant ship, the *Jalakania*, along with two lovely Baptist missionary ladies from Assam. For six weeks we were cruising around the shores of India, picking up cargo to bring to America. We had plenty of time to rest, pray, read, write, and even play the accordion. I played the few hymns I had learned for our regular Christian services, and also taught Mervin and the second engineer what I knew about playing the accordion.

Things went rather smoothly and we enjoyed going ashore in several places, including Sri Lanka (Ceylon at the time). There we were privileged to hear the loving brother, John Wright Follett, speak during a Sunday morning church service.

The day came when things changed drastically. As we moved out of the Suez Canal into the Mediterranean Sea, we lost one of the ship's propellers and immediately there was chaos all over the ship. For seventeen hours we were at the mercy of the waves.

When it happened, I was on my way from the dining room up to our stateroom on the bridge bringing Mervin her supper because she was not feeling well. The Captain and some of the engineers passed me running at high speed in search for the cause of the trouble. Later, we four women were in prayer in our room, and the Captain and engineers came to request prayer for the situation.

A great storm was heading our way but God turned it and showed His power on our behalf. Hallelujah! The officials kept us posted as to what was happening. We quoted scripture and witnessed to them, so God was glorified in it all. May His Name be praised!

They that go down to the sea in ships, that do business in great waters;

These see the works of the Lord, and his wonders in the deep.

For he commandeth, and raiseth the stormy wind, which liftest up the waves thereof.

They mount up to the heaven, they go down again to the depths: their soul is melted because of trouble.

They reel to and fro, and stagger like a drunken man, and are at their wits' end.

Then they cry unto the Lord in their trouble, and he bringeth them out of their distresses.

He maketh the storm a calm, so that the waves thereof are still.

Then are they glad because they be quiet; so he bringeth them unto their desired haven.

Oh that men would praise the Lord for his goodness, and for his wonderful works to the children of men!

Psalm 107:23-32

This Psalm describes just the way it is, and one has to experience it to really know what it is like to be tossed about on the great waters, and then to feel the great calm God can give.

As soon as the propeller dropped off, the ship began to roll back and forth to a 45 degree angle, tossing dishes and every loose item across the rooms. Both Mervin and I had to lie on the floor between our cots, so there wasn't much sleep for us that night. But everything has an end. The next day, Miss Steven and I were out on deck when we saw a shining vessel coming toward our ship. The sun shining on the metal made it look as though it was lit up with the glory of God. Miss Steven said, "Walking on the water," and tears of joy filled our eyes. It reminded us of Jesus walking on the water to get to His disciples.

Three war ships from Greece came in relays and towed us into Malta harbor, where Paul was shipwrecked. For five days we experienced a "great calm." No motors were operating, so there was no vibration. Glory to Jesus!

Our ship went into dry dock for two months, so the Captain had to see about getting the four missionaries to the states. We were praying and the Lord let me know when we would be leaving the island. We were there four days and an American transport ship changed its course and picked us up at the time appointed by the Lord. Hallelujah!

We had been at sea for two months and had two more weeks of very rough sailing ahead of us in the North Atlantic. We passed the area where the great Titanic went down, being sliced by an iceberg in 1913. One day we were within 50 miles of a huge iceberg. The waters were so rough that even the Captain had to stay in bed for five days. Only those who operated the ship were able to stay up. We ate boiled potatoes and butter from a paper cup that was brought to our rooms for those five days.

Three of us women occupied one room. We could see mountainous waves as high as our ship and could not lie still on our beds. The ship would pitch and roll, pitch and roll. Continually our bodies were kept in movement that would not let up. The monotony of it was almost unbearable. We prayed, we sang, and we tried to encourage one another in the Lord. He was our only hope and we found refuge in Him. Praise His Name!

Finally, we passed through the rough waters and enjoyed some days in more peaceful circumstances. The Chief Steward and Captain were very kind gentlemen. They invited the four of us to dine with them on the bridge four times during the two weeks voyage and we had great times witnessing the things of God to them.

When the going was so rough, the Chief Steward had told us that the only encouragement he could give us was that we could tell our friends we had been at sea at its worst. He said that the last ship they were on broke in two in the middle.

The day we were leaving Halifax, the Captain and Chief Steward asked us to pray that the water would not be rough on the last leg of our voyage down the coast to

New York. We prayed, and all the way down the water was as smooth as glass. What a great God we have!

What a thrill it was to hear the words, "We are coming into harbor." I walked out on deck where many of the passengers were standing. There before us was the Statue of Liberty. Tears began to flow down my face very unexpectedly. I felt embarrassed but as I glanced around, I saw that everybody was weeping. A steward who was standing by said, "Don't feel embarrassed. We shed tears each time we come in from a trip." That was every month.

When the reporters came on board and asked the Captain if he had any important people on the ship, he sent them to us. So, the Lord opened the way for us to tell of the great experiences He had brought us through during these ten weeks at sea. To Him be the glory!

Chapter 14
And the End is Not Yet

The angel of the Lord encampeth round about them that fear him, and delivereth them.

Psalm 34:7

Time goes on and so does the work of the Lord. I started writing this book many years ago, when the experiences were fresh in my memory. However, since I was continually preoccupied with the work of the ministry, my schedule didn't allow much time for writing. I told someone that I was too busy making history to write it. My main purpose now is to encourage people to trust the Lord in times of need. What He has done for one, He will do for another, as they trust and obey Him. That is the secret of victory.

We're living in the end time, and many unusual events are taking place, both good and bad. The enemy would like to keep our minds filled with fear, but our God is greater than anything that could happen to us. There is no fear in God, and He has not given us a spirit of fear. He often said to His disciples, "Fear not."

There was a time in India, I recall, when the enemy attacked me with a spirit of fear. It was during my second term, and not long after the "Great Calcutta Killings" that took so many lives. Juanita and Mervin had gone to Darjeeling in the mountains for some time to get away from the terrific heat. It was tourist season in Darjeeling, and there seemed to be no place for them to stay. However, the Lord provided a room in a lovely lady's home, and an attic room became available in the same home.

Juanita and Mervin wrote to me suggesting that I join them and take a break from the severe heat. When I received the letter, it seemed impossible for me to go, because I was told that there were riots all over Calcutta. Even in Puri, there were robberies in broad daylight. Our lives were in danger wherever we were, but my faith was in God believing that He would protect me. There was no way that I was able to make myself safe in our house. I was well aware of the peril of traveling through the city of Calcutta, and changing railway stations in order to continue on to Darjeeling by train. Not only were the city streets dangerous, but gangs were invading the train and killing passengers. All of this was even more complicated by the fact that I didn't have the money for my fare.

The enemy did his best to put a spirit of fear on me. I asked the Lord (providing it was His Will for me to go to Darjeeling) if he would first of all supply the fare, and secondly deliver me from all fear. I didn't have long to wait. A letter came from America with more than enough to meet my expenses, and as I prayed, the Lord removed all fear. I felt that I could cross Calcutta safely, even if I were surrounded with riots. Glory to Jesus!

When I reached Calcutta, I found there was no rioting. I was unable to reserve a berth on the train, so I asked the Lord to reserve one for me. When I arrived at the station, I learned that the compartment reserved for missionaries was fully booked except for an upper berth near the door. That was fine for me, especially since the

Lord had a soldier standing guard at the door all night long. Hallelujah!

Needless to say, I reached my destination without incident. My attic room was absolutely priceless. I was able to lie on my bed and gaze at the beautiful, everlasting snows on the famous Kinchenjunga mountain, third highest in the world. I'm sure that the saying is true, "When the Lord *guides*, He *provides*."

Fear tried to take hold of me on another occasion some time after the robbery in Kanpur mentioned earlier. Some of the missionaries' sons were in camp, preaching in a village not far from the mission station at Jasidih Junction, where I was staying. One night, some robbers attacked them, forcing them to break camp and come home. Hearing their story brought back memories of the robbery I had so recently experienced. Even though the Lord had already protected me and kept me from fear during the attack, fear came in full force afterwards and I was in terror that someone might break into my room at any moment. I called on the Lord, and He answered me in a unique way. He built up my faith by asking me questions. He asked me, "If you had a night watchman outside, would you be afraid?"

I answered, "No, I would not be much afraid."

"If you had a police force patrolling the house, would you be afraid?" He asked after my response.

I said, "No, Lord, I wouldn't be afraid."

Then He asked, "If you had an army of soldiers surrounding the house, would you be afraid?" I was beginning to see what He was doing. He topped it off with this question, "If all the armies of the world were stationed around the house, would you be afraid?" I began to laugh and rejoice. He said, "You have greater protection than that." My fears were gone. Hallelujah!

71

The angel of the Lord encampeth round about them that fear him, and delivereth them.

Psalm 34:7

Many other fearful situations presented themselves in India, but the Lord never failed me. I remember walking in my compound near the Indian preacher's quarters, carrying an Indian child in my arms. There was no apparent danger, but I happened to look up, and about six feet from me was a large baboon sitting on the brick wall. He dwarfed the chattering monkeys that were usually found playing leap frog around the wall of the compound on Sunday mornings while we were in the prayer room. I should have known better, but this beast looked vicious and I said, "You ugly thing!" Instantly, with a wicked look, he leaped off the wall and headed toward us. It seemed to be a moment of life or death, but Jesus never fails. Just in time, the Indian preacher with his companion came into the compound walking toward his quarters. He perceived the danger, and took care of the situation. Praise the Lord!

God is our refuge and strength, a very present help in trouble.

Psalm 46:1

Fear comes in a variety of packages. Another time of danger involved an Indian child, but this time it was with a snake. A servant's baby was lying under a little improvised tent we made in a cool place out in the yard. I happened to pass by and noticed a large snake was slithering toward the child. The makeshift tent was positioned in such a way, that it was impossible to reach the child without first encountering the snake. There was no object nearby for me to use to either remove or kill the snake. I cried out and a servant came quickly. I don't remember how he did it, but the baby's life was saved and the snake was removed. I give God the glory for this miracle of deliverance.

This brings to remembrance another time I first arrived in India and a poisonous snake found its way into my bedroom. A servant destroyed it, but it surely left quite an impression on me to say the least. I also awoke one night to see a large stinging scorpion on my bedroom wall less than six inches from my face. By the Lord's help, I was able to deal with the creature myself. Praise His Name! The Lord is faithful to spread His wings over His children to protect them all from danger (Psalm 91).

These are but a few surprises the enemy tries to spring on someone on the mission field to cause discouragement and defeat. However, God is mighty and faithful to take care of His servants who trust in Him and obey His Word. The triumphs over circumstances and the joy of winning souls for Jesus far outweighs anything that could ever happen to us. Glory to God forevermore!

Epilogue

Where are they all now? Upon our arrival to the United States, Mervin Arnold continued her education and went on to become a teacher. Juanita Boory, a truly consecrated and devoted Christian who remained to continue the ministry in India has gone on to be with Jesus. The Lindens have also finished their race. They leave a legacy of greatness in the service of missions to the glory of the Lord.

In another book, entitled *500 Miles of Miracles in India*, I wrote further accounts of the Linden family, who were with me in Puri, India. As indicated in the foreword of this book, Aubrey Phillips spent time at the Puri mission, where he met Dorothy Linden. It was also here that Aubrey received confirmation of his call to the ministry. After years of schooling for both of them, and more years of worldwide career related travel for Aubrey, they were joined in marriage.

With his position, Aubrey was transferred by his company to several countries and was used by God to minister wherever he was sent. Upon his retirement from his secular career, he was called to the United States to pastor a church in Michigan.

After serving as pastor for eight and a half years, he and Dorothy moved to Blairsville, Georgia, a mere twenty-five miles from our home. I boastingly say,

"They met as teenagers in my home in India, and now, as grandparents, they live just twenty-five miles from me here in the Smokey Mountains." Praise the Lord!

The blessing of the Lord, it maketh rich, and he addeth no sorrow with it.

Proverbs 10:22

Since my return to America, my ministry was far from over. I married Rev. Robert L. Jenkins. We have had decades of ministry together literally around the world including India, providing prolific material for another book.

They that sow in tears shall reap in joy.

He that goeth forth and weepeth, bearing precious seed, shall doubtless come again with rejoicing, bringing his sheaves with him.

Psalm 126:5,6

He sent some forth to sow where fields were barren;
And some He sent to reap where they had not sown,
But on that day when all the sheaves are garnered,
We'll all rejoice together around God's glorious Throne.

— Pearl Ballew Jenkins

Other Books by Pearl Ballew Jenkins

My Vision of Heaven and Hell
This book tells of an astounding vision of heaven and hell experienced by the author in 1932. The vision is recorded in vivid detail, and has blessed countless people for well over fifty years.

500 Miles of Miracles in India
This is the author's testimony of the the miraculous power of Almighty God to protect and provide for His own in the face of extraordinary danger. This book tells of a five hundred mile journey the author traveled while serving in India as a missionary. It will inspire and encourage your heart to believe God for the supply of every need.

Copies of these books can be obtained from:

Rev. Robert Jenkins
P.O. Box 8
Murphy, N.C. 28906
or
A Great Love, Inc.
P.O. Box 1248
Toccoa, Georgia 30577